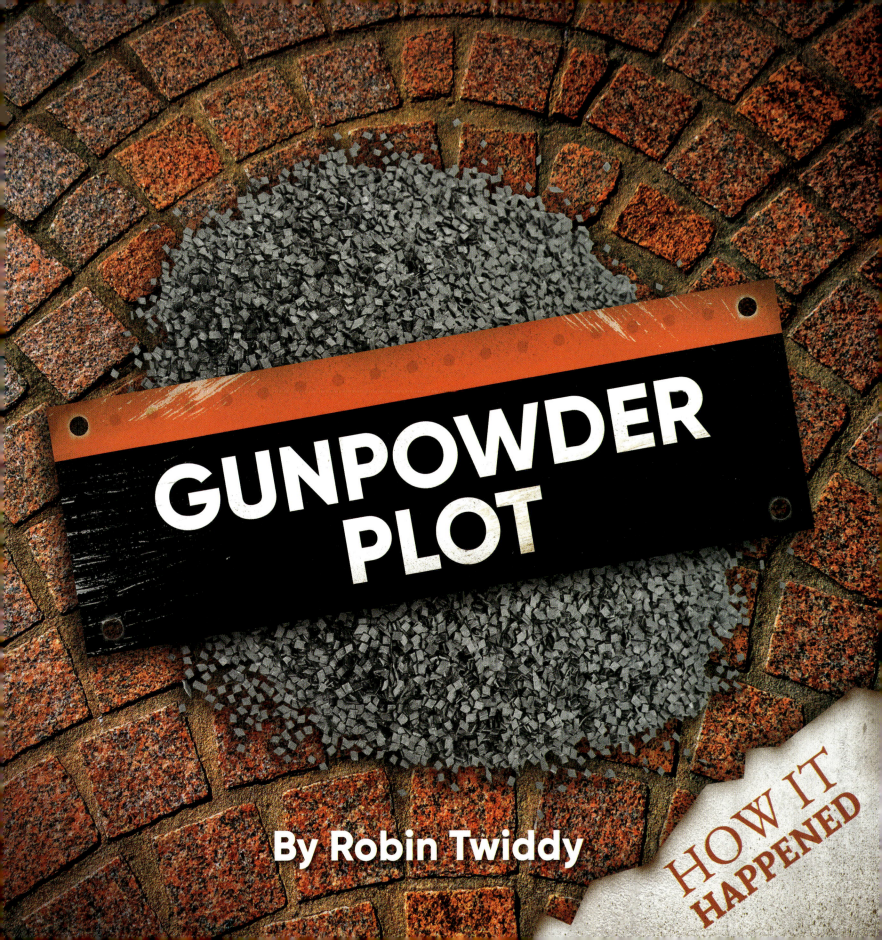

GUNPOWDER PLOT

By Robin Twiddy

HOW IT HAPPENED

BookLife PUBLISHING

©2021
BookLife Publishing Ltd.
King's Lynn
Norfolk PE30 4LS

ISBN: 978-1-83927-448-0

Written by:
Robin Twiddy

Edited by:
Madeline Tyler

Designed by:
Gareth Liddington

A catalogue record for this book
is available from the British Library.

Photo credits:

Front Cover – Brad Summerson, milart, koya979, MarkophotoLC, Carlos Amarillo, Vitezslav Halamka, 2&3 – Sven Hansche, 4&5 – Cristian Gusa, Everett Collection, 6&7 – Rido, Zivica Kerkez, anakband, 8&9 – Didecs, Connormah, AlexSmith, Crispijn van de Passe, the Elder, Kigsz, revers, 10&11 – David Levy, macondo, Andrei Mayatnik, Mega Pixel, Chinnapong, 12&13 – Kigsz, Lotus_Studio, Nicholas Piccillo, Vasyl90. Parrot of Doom, 14&15 – Paladin12, Pakhnyushchy, 16&17 – Dietmar Rabich, donsimon, ratsadapong rittinone, Charles Gogin, Trelleek, 18&19 – Picsfive, ArtMari, 20&21 – LianeM, Beautiful landscape, Big Foot Productions, 22&23 – Cat_arch_angel.

Images are courtesy of Shutterstock.com. With thanks to Getty Images, Thinkstock Photo and iStockphoto.

CONTENTS

Words that look like <u>this</u> can be found in the glossary on page 24.

PARLIAMENT AND THE LAW

Laws are sets of rules that everyone agrees to live by. Laws should help and protect the people they are made for. In England, laws are made by Parliament.

1603
James I becomes King

Parliament meets in the Houses of Parliament.

James I became king of England in 1603. James I and Parliament made laws that some people thought were unfair.

Some of the people who were unhappy came together to plot against King James.

King James I

RULES AND LAWS FOR YOU

Laws are like rules that we have to live by.
Are there rules at your school or at home
that you have to follow? What are they?

Think about your favourite game. What would happen if it didn't have any rules?

Think about a rule you have at home or school. Now get into a group with your friends or classmates. Talk about why you might have this rule.

Here are some things to think about:
- Is the rule fair?
- Who does it help?
- What might happen if you didn't have the rule?

THE PLOT

Guy Fawkes and his friends didn't <u>agree</u> with some of the laws made by King James I and Parliament. They made a plot to blow up the Houses of Parliament.

Guy Fawkes – the gunpowder expert

Robert Keyes – looked after the gunpowder

The plan:

- Hire a <u>cellar</u> under the Houses of Parliament
- Buy 36 barrels of <u>gunpowder</u>
- Hide the barrels under Parliament
- Blow up King James I and Parliament – Guy Fawkes will do this on the morning of the 5th of November

1603
James I becomes King

May 1604
Plotters meet at the Duck and Drake

Robert Catesby – the man with the plan

John Grant – bought weapons for the plot

MAKE A GUY FAWKES HAT

You will need:

Scissors (and an adult)

Black card

Silver card

Glue or tape

STEP 1

Roll a piece of black card around your head in a tube shape. Glue the edges together.

STEP 2

Place the tube on another piece of black card and draw around it. Cut this circle out of the card and tape it to the top of the tube.

STEP 4

Tape the rim to the bottom of the tube.

STEP 3

Take the card with a hole in it and cut the edges into a circle. This is the rim.

STEP 5

Draw a buckle shape on the silver card, cut it out and glue it to the front of the hat.

Now get plotting!

11

WHAT WENT WRONG?

Guy Fawkes did not blow up Parliament. He was caught on the night of the 4th with long matches in his pocket, 36 barrels of gunpowder and a guilty look on his face.

So, what went wrong?

1603
James I becomes King

May 1604
Plotters meet at the Duck and Drake

26th October 1604
Lord Monteagle gets a letter warning him not to go to Parliament

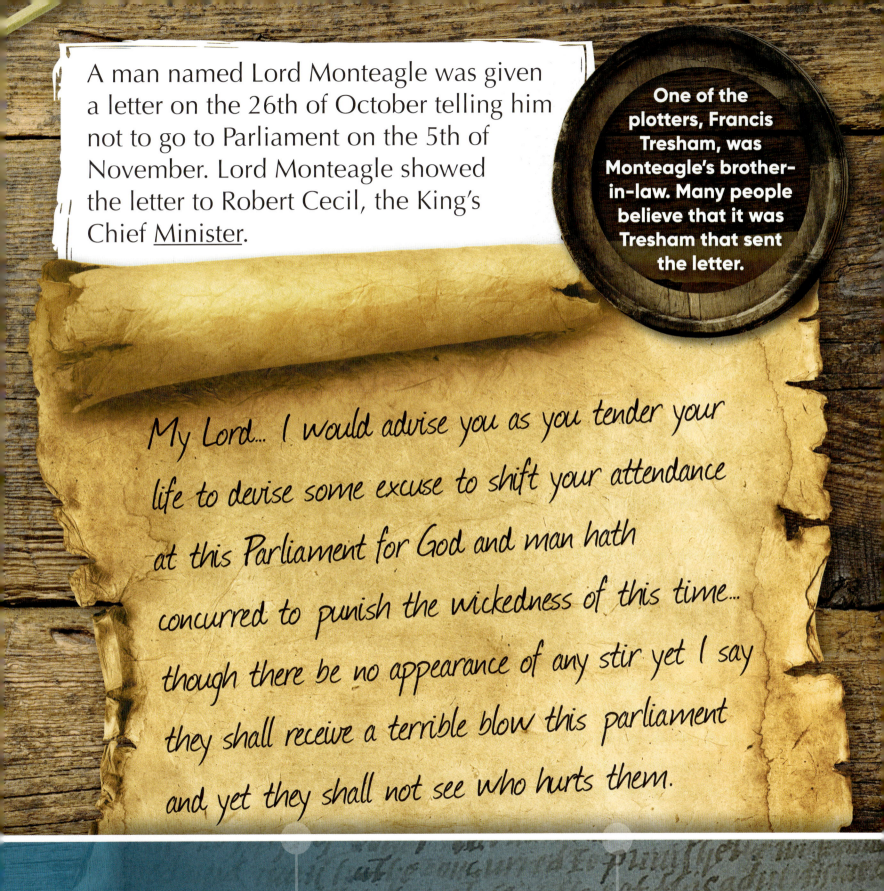

A man named Lord Monteagle was given a letter on the 26th of October telling him not to go to Parliament on the 5th of November. Lord Monteagle showed the letter to Robert Cecil, the King's Chief <u>Minister</u>.

One of the plotters, Francis Tresham, was Monteagle's brother-in-law. Many people believe that it was Tresham that sent the letter.

My Lord... I would advise you as you tender your life to devise some excuse to shift your attendance at this Parliament for God and man hath concurred to punish the wickedness of this time... though there be no appearance of any stir yet I say they shall receive a terrible blow this parliament and yet they shall not see who hurts them.

WRITE A LETTER

Now it is time to write a letter to Lord Monteagle to warn him not to go to Parliament.

You will need:

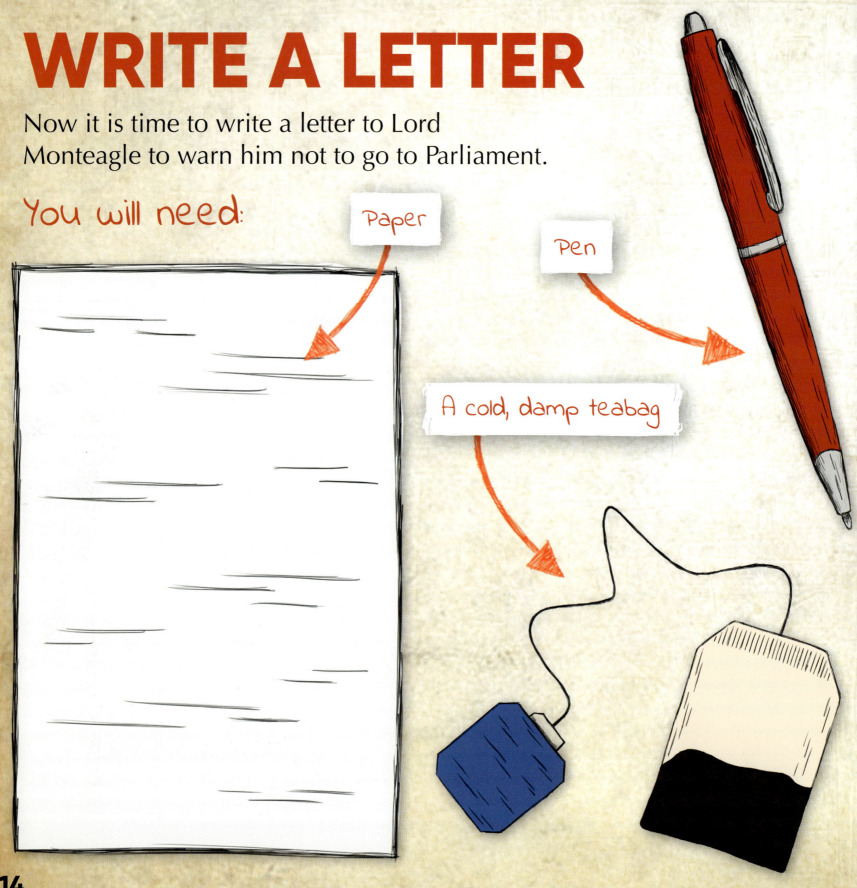

Paper

Pen

A cold, damp teabag

WRITE YOUR LETTER...

Things to include:

- What should Monteagle avoid?

- When?

- Don't forget to ask him not to show anyone the letter.

If you want to, you can copy the letter from page 13.

When you have written your letter, it is time to make it look old.

- Tear a corner or two off your letter

- Now take your damp, cold teabag and pat it onto your paper gently. This should turn the paper yellow and brown.

Guy Fawkes was taken to the King himself. When asked what he was doing, Fawkes answered, "I wish to blow the Scottish King and all of his Scottish Lords back to Scotland."

1603
James I becomes King

May 1604
Plotters meet at the Duck and Drake

26th October 1604
Lord Monteagle gets a letter warning him not to go to Parliament

Fawkes was taken to the Tower of London where he was tortured until he gave up the names of the other plotters. Guy Fawkes and the other plotters were ordered to be killed for carrying out <u>treason</u>.

This is the White Tower, where Guy Fawkes was held.

TELL THE STORY

Can you place these parts of the story in order? Copy them onto pieces of paper and put them in the correct order.

Robert Catesby, Guy Fawkes and others made a plan.

Guy Fawkes gave up the names of the other plotters.

Lord Monteagle got a letter.

Guy Fawkes was caught with the barrels of gunpowder.

Guy Fawkes was tortured.

King James and Parliament made some laws that Robert Catesby and Guy Fawkes didn't agree with.

Guy Fawkes and the other plotters were sentenced to death.

Lord Monteagle warned the King.

BONFIRE NIGHT

After the King's men caught Guy Fawkes and the other plotters, the King <u>declared</u> that every year on the 5th of November the people of England would celebrate how the plot was stopped.

1603
James I becomes King

May 1604
Plotters meet at the Duck and Drake

26th October 1604
Lord Monteagle gets a letter warning him not to go to Parliament

People have been celebrating Bonfire Night in England for hundreds of years. Talk to your parents, carers and grandparents to see how they used to celebrate it. Is it different to how you do it now?

Remember, remember the fifth of November,
Gunpowder treason and plot.
We see no reason
Why gunpowder treason
Should ever be forgot!

4th November 1604
Guy Fawkes is caught red-handed

5th January 1605
Guy Fawkes is put to death

MAKE A FIREWORKS DISPLAY

Fireworks are one of the best parts of Bonfire Night. Let's make our own fireworks display.

What you will need:

Paintbrush

Brightly coloured paints

A straw

Black paper

How to make a fireworks display

Make sure your colourful paints are runny. Use your paintbrush to put big wet splodges of colour onto your page. Now use your straw to blow in the middle of the splodges. Your paint should spread out like an exploding firework!

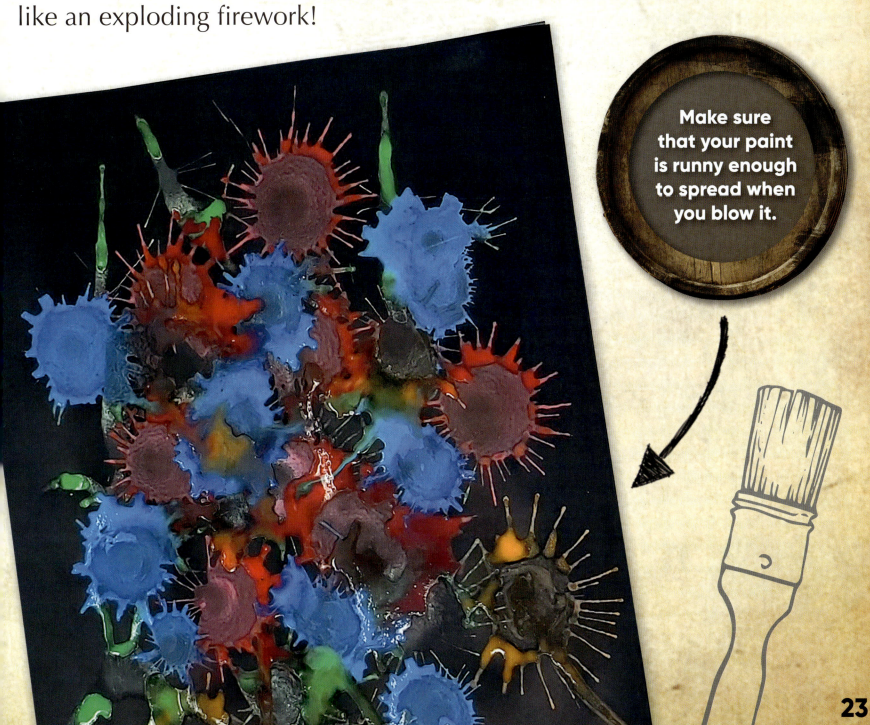

Make sure that your paint is runny enough to spread when you blow it.

GLOSSARY

agree	think or feel the same way
cellar	an underground room usually used to store food and drink that need to be kept cold
declared	to say something in an official way
gunpowder	an explosive powder used to fire guns
minister	someone in charge of a part of the government (the government are the people who run the country)
plot	plan something in secret
treason	a crime against one's own country

INDEX